Title of Your Cookbook

Recipes from the 99, Everyone's Favorite NYPD Precinct

by

Betty Green

Copyright/License Page

Table of Contents

Introduction

Since Brooklyn Nine-Nine came out in 2013, it has done nothing but garners a huge following of audience and fans. That is because the series aims more than just to have a laugh; through the everyday adventures of the New York Police Department, we get to explore the true meaning of friendship, family, love and responsibility.

Of course, the heart of the well-loved sitcom lies in the diverse band of its characters. But food also plays a huge role in many ways! We see some of the detectives bonding as they learn to cook together, while the others have a (friendly but heated) debate over which is the best pie in town.

Just like in real life, the food moments within the show are used to show the growth and depth of different relationships. They include the infamous sourdough started left by Charles' grandmother and the quintessential turkey during one of the Nine-Nine's annual Thanksgiving celebrations.

Title of Your Cookbook sums up all that we love about Jake and Amy's incredible love story, Gina's sarcasm, Rosa's iconic personality and even Terry's hardworking but often hilarious antics.

Not to mention the biggest foodies of the precinct: Hitchcock and Scully! This amusing duo always makes sure to let their love for food known and manages to bring laughter as they do so. From garlic bread and melted ice cream to meatball subs, they know the best way to enjoy these in the office.

Indulge in Captain Holt's healthy but surprisingly tasty smoothie, the perfect steak as Rosa likes it, and Jake's trademark mayonuts sandwich.

Better yet, those wanting to throw a Brooklyn Nine-Nine party can do so simply by following the steps in this cookbook. From refreshing drinks and delicious appetizers to scrumptious dinners and delightful desserts, you will find them all.

Revisit some of the group's most wholesome moments, which include Gina's snarky but genius jokes, Holt's beloved dog Cheddar, and everything in between.

So, are you ready to immerse in the most comedic meal of your life? Let's get started!

1. Holt's Beige Smoothie

Captain Raymond Holt is a stern-faced and stoic captain of the 99th precinct whose diet consists of nutrition bricks and beige smoothies. But despite the outward appearance of someone strict, inflexible and staunchly, he actually has a kind and sweet personality, just like this banana peanut butter smoothie!

Serving Size: 1

Cooking Time: 5 mins

Ingredients:

- Milk - ¾ cup
- Frozen banana - 1
- Peanut butter - 2 tablespoons
- Greek yogurt - ½ cup
- Ground cinnamon - ¼ teaspoon
- Ice cubes as needed

Instructions:

Put all the ingredients in the blender.

Blend until it forms your desired consistency.

Pour into a serving glass and enjoy!

2. Shaw's Bar Tom Collins

Located in the basement of the precinct, Shaw's Bar is a go-to spot for celebration and unwinding for our favorite police squad. It has been the witness to Holt's rare oversharing moments, Jake and Amy's after-party and various job promotions. The bar's signature drink? Tom Collins!

Serving Size: 1

Cooking Time: 5 mins

Ingredients:

- Dry gin – 4 tablespoons
- Simple syrup – 2 tablespoons
- Lemon juice – 2 tablespoons
- Soda – ½ cup
- Ice cubes – 2, extra more for shaking
- Maraschino cherry – 1, for garnishing
- Lemon slice – 1, for garnishing

Instructions:

Shake the dry gin, simple syrup, lemon juice and ice cubes in a shaker.

Strain into a glass with the ice ices and pour the soda.

Garnish with the lemon slice and maraschino Cheers!

3. Hitchcock's Melted Ice Cream

The ice cream is melting! Well, if you are Hitchcock, this is not a problem because the guy turns out to love drinking melted ice cream. In other words, a glass of milkshake. While Hitchcock will drink just about anything served to him, we can assure you that this recipe is really quite delicious.

Serving Size: 2

Cooking Time: 5 mins

Ingredients:

- Vanilla ice cream – 2 cups
- Whole milk – 1 cup
- Vanilla extract – 1 teaspoon

Instructions:

Blend all the ingredients together until smooth.

Serve in a glass and enjoy!

4. Terry Loves Yogurt Parfait

It is not a secret that Terry loves yogurt, as the phrase itself has become the sergeant's most iconic catchphrase. We have seen him enjoy yogurt at his desk numerous times throughout the years, but always plain on its own! Well, we imagine Terry would have loved it even more if someone made him a yogurt parfait like this one…

Serving Size: 2

Cooking Time: 5 mins

Ingredients:

- Vanilla yogurt - 2 cups
- Granola mix – 1 cup
- Strawberries, sliced – 4

Instructions:

Layer 1 cup of the vanilla yogurt, ½ cup of the granola mix and ½ of the strawberry slices in a parfait cup.

Repeat the layers.

Enjoy cold!

5. The 99 Hunger Strike Potato Chips

Remember Hitchcock and Scully went out on a hunger strike and refused to work on the paperwork files? Gina pointed out that they were snacking on potato chips, to which Scully retorted that they did not count because they have no nutritional value. Classic!

Serving Size: 3

Cooking Time: 25 mins

Ingredients:

- Potatoes – 3
- Chili powder – 1 teaspoon
- Salt – ½ teaspoon
- Oil for frying

Instructions:

Peel the potatoes and slice them as thinly as you can.

Rinse in cold water until the water runs clear.

Pat the potato slices dry with a paper towel.

Heat oil until sizzling, then place the potato slices without overfilling.

Fry on medium heat until the potato slices become crispy and golden brown.

Take out and drain from excess oil.

In a large bowl, toss with the chili powder and salt.

Enjoy!

6. Hitchcock and Scully's Garlic Bread

Another favorite from Hitchcock and Scully is garlic bread, which they have been seen to indulge in more than once. This easy recipe is perfect for snacking on as you rewatch some Brooklyn Nine-Nine episodes.

Serving Size: 4

Cooking Time: 10 mins

Ingredients:

- Garlic cloves, crushed - 4
- Butter - 2 tablespoons
- Olive oil - 2 tablespoons
- Crusty bread, sliced – 3 cups
- Parmesan cheese – 3 tablespoons
- Fresh parsley, chopped – 1 handful

Instructions:

Mix the garlic, butter and olive oil in a small bowl. Microwave for 1 minute.

Toast the crusty bread for 2 minutes in the broiler.

Coat with the garlic butter, then sprinkle the parmesan cheese and fresh parsley on top.

Broil again for 1 minute or until golden brown.

7. Hank's Franks Mustard

According to Hitchcock, Hank's Franks serves the greatest mustard, which is essential when it comes to enjoying your hot dogs. This super quick and simple recipe is easy to make and store in the fridge – ready to garnish your meals anytime!

Serving Size: 2 cups

Cooking Time: 15 mins

Ingredients:

- Yellow mustard – 16 oz.
- Ketchup – 1/3 cup
- Sweet pickle relish – 1/3 cup

Instructions:

Combine all the ingredients.

Serve with your favorite hot dogs!

8. New York's Best Hot Dogs

Nobody can deny that Hitchcock and Scully know their hot dogs the best, and the rest of the team acknowledges this. They even come to the duo for insider tips when finding one of their suspects. Well, if you can build your own perfect hot dogs, it should start with this recipe!

Serving Size: 4

Cooking Time: 12 mins

Ingredients:

- Hot dogs – 4
- Olive oil – 2 tablespoons
- Salt – 2 tablespoons

Instructions:

Salt a pot of water and place the hot dogs in it. Bring to a boil.

Heat up the olive oil in a pan.

Place the boiled hot dogs and cook them until brown.

Enjoy!

9. Nana Boyle's Sourdough

Charles is not only a loyal friend and diligent detective, but he is also very much a family man. So, it is quite surprising to everyone when his Great Nana Boyle left Gina a jar of 140-year-old sourdough starter!

Serving Size: 3

Cooking Time: 5 mins

Ingredients:

- Active yeast — ½ cup
- Warm water - 1 ½ cups plus 1 tablespoon
- Flour - 4 cups plus 2 tablespoons
- Sea salt – 2 teaspoons

Instructions:

Mix the active yeast and warm water, then add the flour and sea salt. Cover with a damp towel and set aside for 30 minutes.

Fold the dough into itself 4 times, then let it rest again for 30 more minutes and repeat the folding technique.

Cover and allow to rise for 8 hours in a dry and room-temperature place.

Slightly knead and shape the dough. Let rest for 30 minutes.

Place the dough into a proofing basket and let it sit there for 1 hour.

Before baking, preheat a Dutch oven in the oven to 550 degrees F.

Move the dough into the Dutch oven and bake for 15 minutes.

Let it cool before slicing!

10. Wing Slutz Wings

Wing Slutz is one of Hitchcock and Scully's favorite restaurants, which they have been going to for a long time. This is also where Gio Costa's wife works and eventually becomes a manager after the iconic duo caught the drug dealer.

Serving Size: 3

Cooking Time: 18 mins

Ingredients:

- Flour - 1/3 cup
- Paprika - 2 tablespoons
- Garlic powder - 1 teaspoon
- Black pepper - 1 teaspoon
- Salt - 1 teaspoon
- Butter - 3 tablespoons
- Chicken wings - 10

Instructions:

Mix the flour, paprika, garlic powder, salt and black pepper.

Toss the chicken wings in the flour mixture.

Line the chicken wings on a baking sheet. Place the cut-up butter on top of them.

Bake at 425 degrees F for 30 minutes.

Turn the chicken wings and bake for 15 more minutes.

Serve hot!

11. Breakfast Bar for Jake

We all know just how much Charles loves and adores Jake! But more than that, he also cares about Jake's eating habits and health, which is why he slips a breakfast bar into his hand while he is about to set off to catch a criminal.

Serving Size: 12

Cooking Time: 40 mins

Ingredients:

- Rolled oats - 2 cups
- Honey - ¼ cup
- Flour - ¼ cup
- Peanut butter - ¼ cup
- Milk - ¼ cup
- Vanilla extract - 1 teaspoon
- Cinnamon - ½ teaspoon
- Baking powder - ¼ teaspoon
- Blueberry jam - 2/3 cup

Instructions:

Grind the rolled oats into coarse flour.

Mix the oats with the flour, honey, peanut butter, milk, vanilla extract, cinnamon and baking powder until they form a thick dough.

Place ¾ of the dough onto a baking pan.

Spread the blueberry jam on top.

Place the remaining dough over it.

Bake at 350 degrees F for 22 minutes.

Once cool, slice and enjoy! Or store in the fridge.

12. Amy's Spinach Apple Salad

Amy Santiago is an ambitious and hardworking detective with a penchant for perfection in everything that she does. It is not surprising to find out that Amy also cares about what goes into her body, and this spinach apple salad is one example of the foods she likes to eat. Refreshing and easy to make, but also nutritious!

Serving Size: 4

Cooking Time: 10 mins

Ingredients:

- Toasted walnuts - ½ cup
- Balsamic dressing – ½ cup
- Apple, sliced - 1
- Pear, sliced - 1
- Baby spinach - 3 cups
- Mixed baby greens - 3 cups

Instructions:

Mix all the ingredients except the balsamic dressing together.

Place into individual serving bowls and serve with the dressing!

13. Charles and Holt's Scrambled Eggs

One of Charles' best foodie moments is when Holt asked him to teach him cooking, so he could make something special for Kevin on their anniversary. After a disastrous yet hilarious scrambled eggs cooking lesson, Holt quitted. However, this ends in a heartwarming and sweet scene.

Serving Size: 2

Cooking Time: 10 mins

Ingredients:

- Eggs – 8
- Salt and black pepper to taste
- Unsalted butter – 2 tablespoons

Instructions:

Lightly beat the eggs.

Season with salt and black pepper.

Melt 1 tablespoon of the unsalted butter over low heat.

Pour the eggs and occasionally stir them as they cook slowly.

It should take around 10 minutes for the eggs to thicken. Make sure the center is still soft for the perfect scrambled egg texture.

Fold in the remaining butter before serving.

Enjoy immediately!

14. Cheddar Cheese Sauce

A Pembroke Welsh Corgi, Cheddar is a cute and clever dog of Holt and his partner Kevin. The two obviously adore and love Cheddar very much, and this cheese sauce recipe is unabashedly inspired by him!

Serving Size: 2 cups

Cooking Time: 10 mins

Ingredients:

- Unsalted butter - 2 tablespoons
- Flour - 2 tablespoons
- Salt - ¼ teaspoon
- Whole milk - 1 cup
- Cheddar cheese, shredded - 1 ¾ cups

Instructions:

Melt the unsalted butter over medium heat. Add the flour, salt and whole milk and mix well.

Cook for 2 minutes, then add the cheddar

Cook until melted.

Serve warm over your favorite dishes!

15. Le Petit Colon Fried Pork Intestine

Rosa's bachelorette parties had been enjoyable, but she declared that Charles had organized the best one. It involves destroying the restaurant known as Le Petit Colon, famous for serving fried pork intestine and other strange dishes!

Serving Size: 4

Cooking Time: 2 hrs. 20 mins

Ingredients:

- Large pork intestine, cleaned - 2 lb.
- Salt – 5 tablespoons
- Dried bay leaves - 5
- Peppercorn – 1 tablespoon
- Vegetable oil - 3 cups

Instructions:

Boil the pork intestine for 15 minutes. Discard the water and boil in clean water for 15 more minutes. Discard the water again.

This time, add 3 tablespoons of the salt, the peppercorn and dried bay leaves.

Cook the intestine over low heat for 1 hour.

Cut and season with the remaining salt.

Let rest for 5 minutes.

Deep fry in the vegetable oil until crunchy.

Serve warm!

16. The PB & J

For the rest of the world, PB & J stands for the classic peanut butter and jelly combo. But for us, fans of Brooklyn Nine-Nine know that it is an acronym for Pontiac Bandit and Jake! The Pontiac Bandit is a car thief that Jake has spent years trying to catch, who also eventually becomes one of his closest frenemies.

Serving Size: 1

Cooking Time: 5 mins

Ingredients:

- White bread slices - 2
- Peanut butter - 2 tablespoons
- Strawberry jam - 2 teaspoons

Instructions:

Spread the peanut butter on one white bread slice.

Spread the strawberry jam on the other white bread slice.

Place the bread slices together to form your sandwich.

Enjoy!

17. Holt's Croque Monsieur

The scene where Charles taught Holt how to cook represents so many nuances about these two characters, including Charles' love for cooking and Holt's sweet and nostalgic side. That is because the captain ended up making a croque monsieur as a nod to his trip with Kevin to Paris.

Serving Size: 4

Cooking Time: 30 mins

Ingredients:

For the Béchamel Sauce:

- Unsalted butter - ¼ cup
- Flour - ¼ cup
- Milk – 1 ½ cups
- Salt and black pepper to taste
- Dijon mustard - ¼ teaspoon
- Nutmeg – a pinch

For the Sandwich:

- White bread slices - 8
- Ham slices - 8
- Emmental cheese, grated – 2 ½ cups
- Parmesan cheese, grated - ¼ cup

Instructions:

To prepare the bechamel sauce, melt the unsalted butter over medium heat. Add the flour, Dijon mustard and milk and cook for 3 minutes.

Season with the nutmeg, salt and black pepper. Set aside.

Spread the bechamel sauce on each white bread slice.

On the 4 white bread slices, place the 2 ham slices and a sprinkle of the cheeses, and close with the other white bread

Top with more of the bechamel sauce and a generous amount of the cheeses.

Bake at 425 degrees F for 6 minutes.

18. Hitchcock and Scully's Burrito

We have all seen either Hitchcock or Scully heat up a burrito in the precinct microwave, which is definitely much better than the toaster oven. According to them, it takes 16 minutes to cook using the latter!

Serving Size: 6

Cooking Time: 45 mins

Ingredients:

- Ground beef – 1 lb.
- Taco seasoning mix – 1 oz.
- Refried beans - 1 ½ cups
- Corn - ¾ cup
- Cooked rice - 3 cups
- Flour tortillas – 6
- Cheddar cheese - 1 ½ cups

Instructions:

Cook the ground beef over medium heat and season with the taco seasoning

Once cooked, set aside.

Assemble the burrito by spreading 1/6 of the seasoned beef, ¼ cup of the refried beans, ½ of the cooked rice, 2 tablespoons of the corn and ¼ cup of the cheddar cheese on one flour tortilla.

Roll and wrap in aluminum foil.

Repeat with the other flour tortillas.

Bake for 25 minutes at 350 degrees F.

Serve!

19. Jake's Traditional Mayonuts Sandwich

One of Jake's favorite pastimes and Thanksgiving traditions is eating "Mayonuts" while watching football. While a spoonful of mayonnaise with nuts may not sound that appetizing for most, we bet that this sandwich version is!

Serving Size: 1

Cooking Time: 5 mins

Ingredients:

- Bread slices – 2
- Mayonnaise - 1 tablespoon
- Peanut butter - 2 tablespoons
- Lettuce leaves – 2

Instructions:

Layer the mayonnaise on one of the bread slices. On the other, spread the peanut butter.

Place the lettuce on top and close the sandwich.

Enjoy!

20. Scully's Meatball Sub

Yes, we do talk about Scully a lot in this cookbook, but that is only because the man really knows his foods! Other than that, he actually was an accomplished detective in his younger years. Plus, did you know that Scully can sing opera and has a dog named after his ex-wife, Kelly?

Serving Size: 4

Cooking Time: 35 mins

Ingredients:

- Frozen meatballs - 16
- Marinara sauce - 2 cups
- Hoagie rolls - 4
- Garlic butter - 4 tablespoons
- Mozzarella cheese, shredded - 1 cup

Instructions:

Prepare the frozen meatballs according to the package instructions.

Simmer the meatballs with the marinara sauce for 10 minutes.

Spread the garlic butter on each hoagie roll, then broil for 3 minutes.

Place the 4 meatballs on each hoagie roll along with some of the marinara sauce and mozzarella cheese.

Broil for 3 more minutes and enjoy!

21. The One Thing Meatball

Who could ever forget that at one point, Charles opened his own food truck called The One Thing? True to its name, the truck offered only one single menu, which is "the perfect meatball sandwich." Apparently, it is based on his own grandma's recipe, so you know it is going to be good.

Serving Size: 8

Cooking Time: 50 mins

Ingredients:

- Ground beef – 1 lb.
- Ground veal – 1 lb.
- Ground pork – 1 lb.
- Garlic cloves, minced - 2
- Eggs - 2
- Romano cheese, grated - 1 cup
- Parsley, chopped - 1 ½ tablespoons
- Salt and black pepper to taste
- Italian bread, crumbled - 2 cups
- Lukewarm water - 1 ½ cups
- Olive oil - 1 cup

Instructions:

Mix all the meats with the garlic, eggs, Romano cheese and parsley.

Season with salt and black pepper.

Use the food processor to blend the mixture with the Italian Add the lukewarm water, ½ cup at a time.

Shape meatballs.

Fry the meatballs over medium heat in the olive oil until they crisp up a bit.

You are done! Use in your favorite meatball sub sandwich or pasta recipe.

22. Sloppy Jessica

Gina knows best. Everyone in the 99th precinct knows that. We know that. Not only because Gina *does* sometimes know best, but also because she keeps repeating it. Well, it is one of her antics that makes her so quirky and loveable. Bold, bubbly and exciting, Gina is very much like the show's own Sloppy Jessica.

Serving Size: 4

Cooking Time: 50 mins

Ingredients:

- Salt and black pepper to taste
- Olive oil - 2 tablespoons
- Onion, chopped - 1 ½ cups
- Green bell pepper, chopped - ¾ cup
- Garlic cloves, minced - 3
- Chili powder - 3 tablespoons
- Red pepper flakes - ½ teaspoon
- Ground cumin - 1 tablespoon
- Dried oregano - 2 teaspoons
- Ground beef – 1 lb.
- Canned peeled whole tomatoes, chopped, juice reserved – 28 0z.
- Hot sauce - 2 tablespoons
- Elbow macaroni – 1 lb.
- French rolls – 4
- Mozzarella cheese, grated – 1 lb.

Instructions:

Cook the onion and green bell pepper in the olive oil over high heat for 2 minutes. Add the garlic, chili powder, red pepper flakes, ground cumin and dried

Stir for 1 more minute.

Add the ground beef and cook for 7 minutes. Stir occasionally.

Add the canned peeled whole tomatoes and bring to a boil.

Mix with the hot sauce. Season with salt and black pepper.

Simmer for 30 minutes.

Meanwhile, cook the elbow macaroni according to the package instructions, then add it to the chili mixture.

Slice the French rolls and coat with the mozzarella Bake at 425 degrees F for 8 minutes.

Top each French roll with a generous ladle of the chili macaroni mixture.

23. Easy Takoyaki

In one of the episodes, Charles was eating some Takoyaki, when he met and talked deeply with Genevieve. She eventually becomes his lover and the mother of their child! Definitely a savory start to their relationship that is for sure.

Serving Size: 12

Cooking Time: 4 hrs.

Ingredients:

- Flour – 1 cup
- Water – 2 tablespoons
- Egg - 1
- Dashi stock – 1 ¼ cups
- Cooking oil to spray
- Cooked octopus – 1.8 oz.
- Spring onions, chopped - ¼ cup
- Red pickled ginger – 2 tablespoons
- Takoyaki sauce – 2 tablespoons
- Mayonnaise – 1 tablespoon
- Seaweed flakes – 1 tablespoon
- Bonito flakes – 2 tablespoons

Instructions:

Mix the egg, water and dashi stock.

Add the flour and combine well.

Spray a Takoyaki pan with cooking oil

Pour the batter into the Takoyaki holes.

Add one piece of the cooked octopus and some of the spring onions and red pickled ginger into each ball. Add more of the batter until it overflows.

Let cook for 1 minute. Use a stick to flip.

Keep flipping as all sides of the balls cook until they turn golden brown.

Place on a plate. Serve with the Takoyaki sauce, mayonnaise, seaweed flakes and bonito flakes.

Enjoy!

24. Sal'z Pizza

Did you know that Charles always sends out a weekly email ranking different pizza places in the city? What is even more surprising is that Holt always reads it! It turns out that the newsletter ended up helping the gang solve an important case.

Serving Size: 8 slices

Cooking Time: 55 mins

Ingredients:

- Pizza dough – 16 oz.
- Olive oil - 1 tablespoon
- Pizza sauce - 1 cup
- Mozzarella cheese, sliced – 3 oz.
- Mozzarella cheese, shredded – 1 ¼ cups
- Pepperoni – 2.5 oz.
- Parmesan cheese, shredded - 2 tablespoons

Instructions:

Roll out the pizza dough until it forms around a 12-inch circle.

Place on parchment paper.

Spread the pizza sauce, then top with the rest of the ingredients.

Bake at 550 degrees F for 12 minutes until all the cheese melts.

Serve warm!

25. Mama Magglione's Lasagna

When talking about the most iconic foods and dishes from Brooklyn Nine-Nine, it only seems fair to mention Mama Magglione's Lasagna. It has made an unforgettable appearance in the precinct microwave and should be top on your menu list to try!

Serving Size: 12

Cooking Time: 1 hr. 45 mins

Ingredients:

- Lasagna sheets – 12
- Mozzarella cheese, shredded - 4 cups
- Parmesan cheese, shredded - ½ cup
- Ground beef – ½ lb.
- Italian sausage – ½ lb.
- Onion, diced – 1
- Garlic cloves, minced - 2
- Pasta sauce – 36 oz.
- Tomato paste - 2 tablespoons
- Italian seasoning - 1 teaspoon
- Ricotta cheese - 2 cups
- Parsley, chopped - ¼ cup
- Egg – 1
- Any cheese for topping

Instructions:

Cook the lasagna sheets following the package instructions.

Cook the ground beef, Italian sausage, onion and garlic until the meat turns brown.

Add the pasta sauce, tomato paste and Italian seasoning. Cook for 5 minutes.

In a bowl, combine all the cheeses together with the parsley and egg.

In an empty pasta dish pan, pour 1 cup of the meat mixture.

Place the 3 lasagna sheets, 1/3 of the cheese mixture and 1 cup of the meat mixture.

Repeat twice until all the ingredients run out. Save a little bit of cheese for topping.

Cover the pan with some aluminum foil.

Bake at 350 degrees F for 45 minutes.

Serve!

26. Rosa Diaz Perfect Steak

As the tough guy of the precinct, Rosa is known for her mysterious, scary and clever self. It is why a lot of people are terrified of her, but also why they all love her! One of Rosa's favorite foods is steak, and today we will show you how to cook it perfectly…

Serving Size: 4

Cooking Time: 20 mins

Ingredients:

- Ribeye steaks – 2 lb.
- Vegetable oil – ½ tablespoon
- Salt – 1 ½ teaspoons
- Black pepper – 1 teaspoon
- Unsalted butter – 2 tablespoons
- Garlic cloves, quartered - 2
- Rosemary sprig - 1

Instructions:

Season the ribeye steaks with the salt and black pepper before cooking them.

Meanwhile, heat the vegetable oil over medium heat in a pan.

Place the steaks and sear them for 4 minutes.

Flip and cook for 4 more minutes.

Lower the heat and add the unsalted butter, garlic and rosemary. Spoon the liquid over the steaks continuously for around 1 minute.

Let rest for 10 minutes before serving.

27. Full Boyle Thanksgiving Turkey

We all have to acknowledge that Boyle's tendency to act overboard can be quite over the top at times. And he can be clingy when it comes to both his friends and love interests, which Jake likes to call "Full Boyle." But when it comes to preparing a memorable Thanksgiving meal, you can always bet on Charles!

Serving Size: 16

Cooking Time: 3 hrs. 50 mins

Ingredients:

- Whole turkey – 1
- Onion, quartered – 1
- Lemon, quartered - 1
- Apple, quartered - 1
- Rosemary – ¼ oz.
- Fresh thyme – ¼ oz.
- Fresh sage – ¼ oz.

Salt and pepper to taste

- For the Herb Butter:
- Unsalted butter - 1 cup
- Salt – 1 teaspoon
- Black pepper - ½ teaspoon
- Garlic cloves, minced – 6
- Herbs, chopped – take from the ingredients above

Instructions:

Adjust your oven rack, so the whole turkey will sit in the center of the oven. Preheat the oven to 325 degrees F.

Prepare the herb butter by mixing the unsalted butter, garlic, salt, black pepper and 1 tablespoon of each of the rosemary, thyme and sage. (Keep the rest of the herbs for the turkey).

Clean the turkey's cavity and pat it dry.

Season the inside of the turkey with salt and pepper. Stuff with the lemon, onion, apple and remaining herbs.

Add 2 tablespoons of the herb butter inside.

Melt the rest of the herb butter in the microwave and brush it all over the turkey.

Roast the turkey for 15 minutes per pound of its weight.

Let it rest for 20 minutes before you carve and serve it up!

28. Charles' School Pie

In the earlier episodes of the series, Charles was in love with Rosa and had to defend her pie choices even though he hated them. The good thing is that in the end, he ended up schooling the arguing Rosa and Gina about the absolute best pie in town! And Charles called it… Graduating School Pie.

Serving Size: 1 pie

Cooking Time: 2 hrs. 20 mins

Ingredients:

For the Crust:

- Flour - 2 cups
- Unsalted butter - ½ cup
- Sugar - 1 tablespoon
- Salt - 1 teaspoon
- Iced water - ⅓ cup

For the Filling:

- Pumpkin puree – 1.5 cups
- Egg - 1
- Egg yolks - 3
- Condensed milk - 1 cup
- Ginger, grated - ½ teaspoon
- Ground cinnamon - 1 teaspoon
- Ground nutmeg - ¼ teaspoon
- Salt - ½ teaspoon

Instructions:

Combine all the crust ingredients and blend in the food processor.

Form the mixture into a dough and let it sit in the fridge for 1 hour.

Knead the dough and place it on a pie plate.

Meanwhile, mix the pumpkin puree, egg, egg yolks, condensed milk, ginger, ground nutmeg, ground cinnamon and salt.

Pour the mixture onto the crust.

Bake at 350 degrees F for 15 minutes.

Cool for 2 hours before cutting and serving.

29. Holt's Favorite Pie

Who could forget "the great pie-napping of 2017"? When Captain Holt found out that the pie Kevin had brought and placed in his office went missing, he made it his mission to figure out the thief. And yes, using his police-level measures and impressive detective abilities!

Serving Size: 8

Cooking Time: 3 hrs.

Ingredients:

- Store bought pie crusts – 14 0z. each
- Apples, sliced - 6 cups
- Sugar - ¾ cup
- Flour - 2 tablespoons
- Ground cinnamon - ¾ teaspoon
- Salt - ¼ teaspoon
- Ground nutmeg - 1/8 teaspoon
- Lemon juice - 1 tablespoon

Instructions:

Roll out one store bought pie crust onto a pie plate.

For the filling, mix the apples, sugar, flour, ground cinnamon, salt, ground nutmeg and lemon juice.

Pour into the pie crust.

Top with the remaining store bought pie crust. Cut slits onto the top.

Bake at 425 degrees F for 45 minutes.

Time to enjoy!

30. Scully's Chocolate-Covered Strawberry

Scully is a huge fan of fondues, whether cheese or chocolate, and likes to make it known throughout the precinct. One time, he even brought a fully functioning fondue fountain to work. While he likes dipping strawberries into chocolate, why not try combining the two for a more convenient snack?

Serving Size: 15

Cooking Time: 20 mins

Ingredients:

- Strawberries – 2 lb.
- Semisweet chocolate chips – 10 oz.

Instructions:

Melt the semisweet chocolate chips with the double boiler method or in the microwave.

Hold one strawberry by the stem and dip it into the chocolate.

Repeat with all the strawberries, arranging them on a baking sheet.

Place in the fridge for at least 15 minutes or until set.

Enjoy!

Conclusion

For some people, Brooklyn Nine-Nine is just another TV show. But for more of us, it is a comforting place to come back to whenever we need some laugh, encouragement, or just a lighthearted time with our favorite detective team.

From Charles' obstinate loyalty, Jake's heroic jokes, Amy's kind perfectionism and Terry's protective nature to Rosa's emotionless but entertaining mannerism, these various recipes are a gateway to their unique dynamic.

We are all here for a good time, so hopefully, this cookbook can provide you with the secret portal to the 99th precinct. Enjoy!

Announcement

Thank you very much for getting this book. By buying my book you show me that you are ready to learn new skills and I can tell for sure you have made the best decision. I become a recipe writer because I love to share my knowledge and experience so that other people can learn.

What's even more special is that from all the books that are available on the internet today you have mine. With every purchase done it's like a gift to me, proof that I've made the best decision, turning my experience and knowledge into a book.

Still, please do not forget to leave feedback after reading the book. This is very important for me because I'll know how far I have reached. Even if you have any suggestions that you think it will make my future books even more practice please do share. Plus, everyone else that won't be able to decide which book to get next will have real feedback to read.

Thank you again

Your truly

Betty Green

About the Author

The one thing she loves more than cooking is eating. Yes, Betty Green enjoys tasting new dishes and loves to experiment with food. While sticking to the classics is also a thing, she wants to create recipes that people can enjoy daily.

She really understands the struggle of choosing the next lunch or dinner or what they should serve at their parties. So, she makes sure that her recipes are not only great for family dinners, or even a single dish but for parties too.

She always says "I have a strong sense of smell and taste, which gives me an advantage in creating new recipes from scratch".

The best part of Betty's recipes is that they are practical and very easy to make. When she does use ingredients that are not so easy to find or rarely used in cooking she makes sure to explain everything and add a simplified cooking description so that everyone can make them.

Everyone who got a cookbook from her says that she changed their life. Helped them finally enjoy spending time in the kitchen, which even helped them bond stronger with their family and friends.

Well, after all, food is one of the best ways to connect with people whether they make the dish together or they sit down and eat it. There are countless ways food can help you in your life, aside from keeping you fed and healthy.

Made in the USA
Middletown, DE
13 May 2023